ON THE EDGE

BALANCING EARTH'S RESOURCES

Text and photographs by

HOWARD G. BUFFETT

Foreword by former
United States Senator

Paul Simon

ISBN 0-9707385-3-6

Library of Congress Control Number: 2001130645

Printed on 170 gsm Nymolla Art paper
by Tien Wah Press (Pte) Limited
4 Pandan Crescent Singapore

Published by BIOIMAGES®

P O Box 4537

Decatur, IL 62525

E-mail: BioImages@aol.com

Fax: 217.429.0206

www.buffettimages.com

BIOIMAGES® and BUFFETTIMAGES® are registered trademarks.

The images of the animals, birds and reptiles in this book were photographed
on the continent in which they appear (with the exception of the golden lion tamarin,
ring-tailed lemur, rainbow lorikeet and the snow leopard).

Dedicated to the many American farmers
who make up the backbone of rural America,
who are stewards of our land,
conservationists at heart,
and are committed to providing food
for people throughout the world.

Special thanks to my family, especially my wife Devon and son Howie,
for assisting with many of my travels.

In particular, I thank my mother and father, who have always
encouraged my interests.

Also, I wish to thank:

Jorge Andrade, Saleem Ali, Le Thi Hoang Anh, Dennis Avery, Mary Aylmer, Jill Bauer, Spencer Beebe, Dr. Daniel Blanco, Dr. Herminio Blanco,

Derek Books, Juan Bremer, Miguel Castelino, Tony Clouston, Dave Cooper, Gordon Cox, Perry Dixon, Jim Doherty, John Dowson, John Elwood,

George Forston, Kathryn Fuller and the Staff of WWF, Linda Fultz, Les Garcia, Franzier Gear, Ray A. Goldberg, Gunther and Nancy Golinia, Li Guanghan,

Suhail Gupta, Scott Hancock, Garth Hovell, Estevan Huaman, Maya Ide, Judy Inman, Arun Jain, Li Jiashun, Jean Keene, Peter Kinnear, Paul Laing,

Teresa Lanum, Bob Little, Anton Louw, Dr. Nick Lunn, Angela Mason, Reiko Mikumo, Karla Miller, Steve Miller, Benjamin Musisi, Bruce Ochse,

Sheldon Olivier, Jane Olson, Emmanuel Opong, Dan Pedersen, Dionisio Raimundi, Wade Roberts, Paul Simon, Richard Siwela, Craig Sloan, Tom Sloan,

Todd Sneller, Alan Strachan, Dr. Ian Sterling, Meg Symington, Dorian Tilbury, Doug Trent, Ann van Dyk and the staff of De Wildt Cheetah and Wildlife Trust,

Dave and Shan Varty, Molly Wilson, Shirley Xia, Goh Bak Yan, Bob Zhang, and Chelsea Zillmer

Without their help and support I could not have produced this book.

CONTENTS

Today nearly one billion people lack access to adequate nutrition. It is estimated that 75 million new individuals will need to be fed each year. This additional consumption, combined with increased affluence, will create significant pressure on food production abilities. The challenge will be how to meet these new food demands while maintaining our natural resource base. [(LEFT) UGANDA — (RIGHT) VIETNAM]

FOREWORD

It is apparent to a non-photographer like myself that Howard Buffett has a keen eye for a picture subject. It is also apparent to those of us who know him—and it will become apparent to the reader—that Howard Buffett also has a keen sensitivity for the human condition, for those who struggle against great odds, and for humanity's future.

This book combines those two attributes with two others. Howard is a farmer, some would say "a gentleman farmer" because he is not dependent on farming for his livelihood. But the term "gentleman farmer" does not portray his role accurately. He gets on that tractor and runs the combine and enmeshes himself in the dust and dirt and practical problems that farmers face. He understands farming.

At the same time he is widely known for his photographs of nature, of a polar bear with her cubs, of birds in tropical forests. He has a sensitivity to the environment and a protective concern about how we are shaping our future through the use and misuse of nature.

All these interests combine in this book.

His observations on conservation and biodiversity have been published in newspapers as varied as the Washington Post and the Wall Street Journal, from conservation publications to the Chicago Tribune.

The call in this book is for a balanced approach to our problems of feeding humanity and saving our planet, with its great diversity of wildlife and plant life.

The timely warning on the pages that follow are valuable because of their brevity and clarity. Thanks to Howard's skills, we both read the message and see the message.

We should heed the warning signals he is sending to us.

Paul Simon
Former United States Senator

Consumption of the world's natural resources has accelerated worldwide. [VIETNAM]

PREFACE

In a society where living on credit is common and spending more than earnings leads to financial insolvency, it is no wonder we are struggling with our environment. We pollute water we cannot cleanse, plow soil that blows in the winds and strip forests we cannot replace. We have abused nature's credit, and we must clear up our debt to avoid environmental bankruptcy. If we are to accomplish this while continuing to feed a growing world population, solutions will have to be global in nature. It is an investment we must make to safeguard our environmental prosperity.

We need to develop long-term sustainable policies addressing the vulnerability of our natural resources and recognizing the value of conservation. The methods needed to preserve these resources while providing for food demands will vary geographically. Developing the policies to achieve these goals is one of the greatest challenges in this new century.

It will be critical to consider local factors, assess the value of our resources in a different manner and take into account the global impact of these decisions. But in the long run, the ultimate success of integrating people's needs and preserving our natural resources will require different attitudes and different actions. "Environmentalism" must make the transition from a cause to a way of life; it must go beyond the dedication of a few and become part of mainstream society.

How do we preserve our natural resources, feed a growing population and incorporate technology in a "sustainable" manner? To be successful in meeting these challenges, we will need to view agricultural production as part of a global risk assessment, utilizing the best suited acreage and most efficient systems to help preserve unique ecosystems. Our policy must discourage agricultural growth which

destroys our biodiverse assets as it expands into virgin forests and jungles. This book discusses one aspect of integrating the preservation of our natural resources with food production. The photography illustrates the pressures humanity has put on our resources and the animal species we stand to lose if we do not modify our current behavior.

Someone once told me, "No one will starve to save a tree." After observing people's behavior in over 45 countries, I know this is true. We need to provide creative alternatives and new solutions to old problems. This book seeks to clearly illustrate the urgency of these global challenges. It provides insight into potential solutions, and visually demonstrates what is at stake if we do not act more responsibly.

Howard G. Buffett

9

American agriculture is one of the safest and most reliable food systems in the world. Based on per capita income, this system is also one of the most efficient for consumers. In addition, it has been the only category of U.S. exports to consistently provide a positive trade balance. While achieving these goals, American agriculture has provided food for millions of people around the world and has been a large contributor to global conservation.

For many years, U.S. agriculture has been viewed as the world's most reliable supplier of agricultural products. However, in the 1970's, politics interfered with normal U.S. agricultural exports. The U.S. grain embargoes imposed on the Soviet Union sent a new signal to the world. The United States was willing to use its powerful food production system as a political weapon. This policy decision not only impacted America's farmers, it gave other countries an opportunity to replace the production relinquished by the U.S. As a result, expansion into new undeveloped areas occurred at an incredibly fast rate. This new crop production in other countries required the clearing of millions of acres, much of which had historically been forestland. Once this process began, it continued indefinitely. As embargoes weakened U.S. exports, the "fence-row to fence-row" planting in the U.S. was replaced with various government set-aside programs in order to reduce production. Our credibility and reliability as a world food provider was undermined and it was an unusual opportunity for other countries to increase their own agricultural production.

The grain embargoes were devastating to conservation, as millions of acres of foreign jungle were destroyed to provide the level of crop production previously supplied by the United States. Later, in the 1980's the U.S. government began to expand its policy of production controls. In addition to the mandatory set-aside required for farmers already participating in other government programs, the government implemented the Conservation Reserve Program (CRP). The number of acres enrolled in the CRP now exceeds 30 million acres, with a goal of 40 million acres. These programs alone cost the U.S. government over $1.5 billion a year in payments.

The majority of CRP acreage can be productive farmland. The increased use of terracing, tiling, grass waterways and no-till farming practices, combined with a more targeted set-aside program focusing on buffer strips, filter strips, wetlands and partial field enrollment would achieve important environmental goals. This would allow a large portion of the land which is currently idle to contribute to global food needs. The use of this acreage would also reduce the need to bring new land into production, some at the expense of virgin forest and jungle.

While the embargo policy took its toll on our credibility as a supplier and allowed new acreage to be put into production elsewhere in the world with heavy environmental costs, the set-aside programs had other effects in the United States. They began to put more pressure on rural America. U.S. agriculture has provided the world's most efficient food system as a result of infrastructure, research, technology, investment, production, transportation, storage and exports. This sophisticated system requires the proper support.

Rural America is more than social fabric; it provides the support system for U.S. agriculture to remain efficient and competitive. It provides the human capital that is the ingenuity that drives a complex inter-relationship between the land, production, marketing and conservation. As this human capital diminishes, so does our ability to remain efficient and independent.

Rural America has a unique value in terms of its highly productive capacity. However, for this capacity to remain intact, rural areas must remain healthy, which means farms must remain economically viable. Rural areas must also have the same access to health care, education and other services which are more easily accessible in urban communities. The solution to these issues is not larger farms or bigger operators. This will only defeat efforts to improve conservation measures at the local level and force consolidation of rural communities, thereby impacting the long term viability of rural areas. Hopefully, emerging technologies will afford new access and opportunities for medium and small scale farms to be more competitive in a global world so rural America can maintain a balance in the scale of production.

A difficult challenge to overcome is that farmers provide an immense value to our society and economy but rarely receive the benefits of this contribution. One reason is that many of these benefits are intangible; they are difficult to quantify and do not always convert into economic gain. A key contribution, often overlooked, is conservation. This book attempts to identify some of the value created by the American farmer in the area of global conservation. It is driven by my love for the land, both as a farmer and as a conservationist. Many would see these as conflicting interests, but I would argue they are not. A system of focused, efficient food production on the most appropriate land prevents the clearing and destruction of other land which has higher ecological value.

The challenge is fitting the pieces together so we can accomplish both of these objectives. It is a bold undertaking that requires global initiatives and a sensitivity to local cultures. We can not expect future generations to resolve these issues. It is our responsibility, and we must act now.

Low yield agricultural production in developing countries is often found in watershed basins, on steep slopes or on marginal land. Such developments often have a negative impact on the surrounding ecosystem. [GHANA]

THE CURRENT CHALLENGE

During this century there will be a balancing act between feeding billions of additional people and maintaining our environmental resources. At the current growth rate of 1.7 percent annually, world population is projected to increase from six billion to eleven billion in 50 to 80 years. Increased food needs will place greater pressure on global natural resources.

Today, the world's farmers are producing crops on about six million square miles, approximately the same amount used in 1950 when the population was half its current level. Without the increased output of high-yield agricultural production (the use of commercial fertilizer, technology, hybrid seeds, irrigation and modern equipment) an additional 10 million square miles of cultivated land would have been needed to achieve our current level of food production. To put this into perspective, 10 million square miles is about 6.5 billion acres, or about 21 times the acreage currently used to produce crops in the United States. A large portion of this area would have

Production that took a U.S. farmer from sunrise to sunset in 1950 now takes less than one hour. [UNITED STATES]

In some countries, such as Vietnam, Cambodia and Thailand, the population is increasing at an alarming rate. Worldwide these countries will be the battleground between population growth and consumption of natural resources at an unsustainable rate. [VIETNAM]

It is estimated that agriculture must triple its output by 2050 to meet the global demand resulting from increased affluence and a larger population. [UNITED STATES]

Feeding a growing population without destroying our natural resource base is perhaps the single greatest challenge we face today. [(LEFT) CHINA — (RIGHT) INDIA]

been taken from forestland, wildlife habitat, wetlands and other valuable ecosystems.

High-yield farming, through increased efficiency, will continue to help protect additional land from cultivation. These gains will come through improved crop varieties, the use of precision farming, application of integrated pest management, the use of global positioning systems (GPS) and increased conservation tillage. GPS will allow farmers to be more precise in the application of fertilizer and herbicides by using a sophisticated satellite system. This will provide a way to map their fields and make applications by computers that interface with these satellites. The success of these approaches in helping to preserve additional wildlife habitat will require international public policy which encourages production on land best suited for agricultural purposes. These policies will allow the American farmer to play an increasingly vital role in both food production and conservation as we move into this century.

World leaders are now assessing environmental issues on a global basis. Largely ignored 10 or 20 years ago, these issues have become the subject of important policy today. The first international convention on biodiversity (1992) focused on the importance of preserving our global natural resources. These efforts directly affect agriculture since fewer than 20 plant species produce 90 percent of the world's food supply. Just three of these plant varieties, corn, wheat and rice, supply over half the current food requirements. Our understanding of the world's biological resources and the consequences of our impact on them is critical to the future balance and maintenance of our food system. Conserving and sustaining the earth's natural resources must remain one of our highest priorities. How agriculture is perceived and the role it plays will largely determine our success in preserving many of these resources.

Sufficient quantities of food do not guarantee its adequate distribution. As a result, poverty and hunger are a primary driver of resource depletion. Hunger is caused by a number of complex issues — from politics and logistics, to economics and greed. Millions of people, half of them children, go to bed hungry every night. Some estimates put this number at a

(TOP) For every acre idled in the United States it can require as much as three or four acres of production elsewhere in the world to meet the same yields.

(MIDDLE) Currently, new births throughout Asia are about 25,000,000 per year, the equivalent of adding another Taiwan every 400 days. It is estimated that Asia will account for about 60% of the total population growth in the next 10 years. [INDIA]

(BOTTOM) Poverty and despair make it impossible for people to consider long term conservation goals. [INDIA]

billion people. The amount of production alone cannot solve all these issues, however policies that reduce agricultural production will exacerbate this problem. It is critical that the environmental community and the agricultural community work in partnership to apply the advantages of high-production agriculture to the benefit of preserving our natural resources, as well as reducing hunger. Neither farmers nor environmentalists alone can eliminate all the problems that cause hunger, but it is our ethical and moral responsibility not to compound the problem. Biodiversity and high-yield agriculture can co-exist, and must, if we are to provide adequate food for the future.

(THIS PAGE) As a result of poor infrastructure, primitive drying techniques lead to a higher likelihood of crop spoilage. [VIETNAM]

(OPPOSITE) In many rural areas, no available resource goes unused. In the mountains of China, a young girl drags corn stalks home to be used as fuel for cooking.

Famine occurs in many developing countries where crops are inconsistent due to flooding and drought. [GHANA]

While abundant crops are raised in the United States, political, logistical and distribution challenges prevent basic food needs from being met in other areas of the world.

A young boy clutches two ears of corn, perhaps the only food he will have that day. [UGANDA]

Children using old vegetable oil cans, haul water home to use in preparing the dinner meal. In this area, poor water quality causes a number of serious diseases, including Guinea worm, elephantiasis and river blindness. [GHANA]

THE VALUE OF BIODIVERSITY

New discoveries from ecological assets have the potential to contribute to even greater agricultural yields. At the heart of all ecological systems is biological diversity. Biodiversity is not something farmers talk about at the local coffee shop. It is, however, already a very important component of their profession. Nature provides a whole system that makes farming viable. Certain species are natural enemies to pests, while others degrade residue, fix nitrogen, help form soil tilth or pollinate crops. A productive and sustainable agricultural system depends on maintaining the integrity of this biodiversity. One of the best lessons U.S. farmers had regarding their reliance on nature's contribution to adaptation occurred in the 1970's. The Southern Cornbelt endured a devastating disease

(THIS PAGE, TOP) In China, every available piece of arable land is utilized to feed over a billion people.

(THIS PAGE, BOTTOM) Tropical climates provide for lush forests. These climates are also ideal for the production of a number of crops. [MALAYSIA]

(OPPOSITE) Ironically, as diverse ecosystems are being consumed by inefficient farming methods, U.S. policy makers debate whether to idle some of the most productive farmland in the world. [VIETNAM]

A young child pitches in to help weed a hand-sown field of corn. [VIETNAM]

In some regions, cash crops are planted in any location in which they will grow. In this situation, an annual corn crop is rotated between long-term crops such as banana trees. [CHINA]

In countries where mechanized production is not feasible, reliance is often placed on intensive manual methods. [VIETNAM]

epidemic caused by southern leaf blight fungus. The ultimate salvation of future corn crops was found in diverse varieties resistant to the disease. It was the closest we have come to breakfast without cornflakes.

Biodiversity functions as nature's technology. It is the process by which nature engineers survival and maintains variety. Various plants, animals, micro-organisms and their ecosystems make up biodiversity, an environmental treasure. Its endowment is the means of continued life on earth. As these resources diminish, our future becomes more precarious. To assure a sustainable future, we must protect these treasures from unnecessary and irreversible harm.

On a human level, biodiversity should be valued similar to our individual health. People normally refrain from poor diets, consuming items of unknown origin, or consciously harming themselves. We make such decisions every day by determining the risk and long-term outcome. Our approach to caring for our natural biological assets should be treated with the same caution, respect and common sense. Our body often sends us signals when we treat it improperly. Nature sends her own signals when neglected or mistreated. As with our bodies, a certain amount of neglect can be endured, yet irresponsible and unchecked behavior will inevitably produce degeneration. Biodiversity is essential for maintaining the quality of human life, and this should be reflected in our actions. High yield and efficient agricultural production systems do not need to compete with these goals.

Our discoveries in biological diversity could potentially continue indefinitely. It is critical to recognize this diversity as an asset, not a commodity. Assets must be maintained and properly cultivated to yield benefits in the future. We are still discovering the extent of those benefits. This generation must use reasonable and sustainable approaches to maintain our biodiversity and our policies should support such efforts.

In testimony before the United States Congress, agronomist and Nobel Peace Laureate Norman Borlaug stated, "By sustaining adequate levels of output on land already being farmed in environments suitable for agriculture, we restrain and even reverse the drive to open more fragile lands to cultivation."

Local food production, particularly fruits and vegetables, will not likely be replaced with large production elsewhere. However, future encroachment into virgin jungle and forest for growing crops such as rice, corn and soybeans can be prevented by utilizing more efficient production elsewhere. [VIETNAM]

In Uganda, forested slopes are cleared by hand for tea plantations. Some trees are too large to be removed, so the stumps remain in the field.

Clear-cut logging techniques can be devastating to the surrounding environment and wildlife species. [UNITED STATES]

BALANCING OUR NEEDS

The balance, between feeding an increasing population while maintaining and preserving our biological assets, may be the greatest challenge of the twenty-first century. Compounding the issue is the fact that future societies will also demand a higher-grade diet as they achieve increased income. Through high-yield production agriculture, the American farmer provides an essential tool to meet both of these needs. This efficiency in agricultural production offsets the need to plow new acreage, helping to preserve natural habitats. Some extremely diverse and fragile areas, such as tropical forests, contain an abundance of animal and plant species. Huge portions of tropical forests are lost to agricultural development, the majority of which takes place in developing countries. The loss of these forests threatens diverse habitats and unique ecosystems and ultimately drives some species to extinction.

To slow this encroachment, several initiatives are needed. Larger conservation areas must be established. More sustainable forestry systems should be put in place, including the integration of commercial plantations with undisturbed forestland. To develop long-term economic solutions for local economies, markets must reflect the value of products extracted from natural plants, which exist as a result of unique ecosystems. Just as important is the use of indigenous agro-forestry techniques, processes that adapt to specific and local circumstances to insure long-term viability. There must be global recognition of the value of these resources and support for the use of low-risk acreage to provide for a large portion of food production requirements. Without this combination, it is unlikely that we will curb the growing environmental abuses so prevalent throughout the world.

Since 1950, U.S. agriculture has tripled its output. This was possible because of a number of technological advances. It is reasonable to believe we can continue to use technology to increase production levels. Combined with conservation tillage, these increases can be achieved without negative environmental consequences and will provide an alternative to bringing unnecessary acreage into production. There has also been an increased awareness of the benefits that conservation tillage systems (such as "no-till") offer in improved air quality as a result of carbon sequestration. Minimum tillage offsets part of the production of carbon emissions because untilled soils delay decomposition of residue, thereby storing carbon and reducing the release of carbon dioxide. In this way, no-till farming methods capture more carbon in the soil, reduce airborne emissions and improve soil quality.

As resources become more scrutinized, even where high-yield agricultural systems are extremely efficient, more will need to be done to manage available resources. Crop irrigation is currently an important part of maintaining high and consistent yields. Water conservation will become much more critical. Although only about 15 percent of all cropland is irrigated worldwide, this land accounts for almost 40 percent of world food production. With competing needs, and more pressure on finite water resources, agriculture will need to balance the benefits of irrigation with urban development and wildlife requirements.

Those who argue against high-yield agricultural systems cannot provide alternatives to meet global food demands. There are niche markets for organic production. However, organic production cannot supply the needs of a growing world population, much less meet the current demand for food. Heavy tillage requirements result from reduced chemical and pesticide use and may contribute to soil loss and add to water quality problems in some organic farming systems.

(CONTINUES ON PAGE 31)

Squatters often move into forest areas and develop small plots of land. Here a tarp serves as temporary shelter while the surrounding resources are consumed for subsistent agriculture. [VIETNAM]

A young boy drinks from his cupped hands. In some parts of the world each drop of water is becoming increasingly important to survival. [UGANDA]

New advancements in irrigation systems have helped conserve water resources used for food production. However, as demand for these resources increases, technology must provide ongoing improvements. [UNITED STATES]

THIS PAGE

(FAR LEFT) The use of water resources, whether in large production systems or small-scale farming, will become a highly contested issue in the near future. [VIETNAM]

(LEFT) Today, more than 100 million acres of U.S. farmland are planted using conservation tillage, such as no-till. By leaving the soil undisturbed and crop residue intact, soil erosion is significantly reduced.

(BOTTOM) An Illinois farmer cuts a field of organically grown wheat. To meet the requirements to qualify for organic certification, this production requires an intensive seven-year rotation program, which among other things, is necessary to help maintain fertility levels. His lower than average yields are to some degree offset by the elimination of expenses for pesticide and herbicide. However, the non-use of herbicide requires intensive cultivation to control weeds. Premiums received for organically produced crops also help overcome the financial impact of lower yields. [UNITED STATES]

OPPOSITE PAGE

(TOP) An aerial view of a circle created from a center pivot irrigation system demonstrates the importance of water in crop production. Without irrigation this crop would not be produced in this area. [UNITED STATES]

(BOTTOM) People with little to lose are willing to risk everything in the hope that new claimed land will provide a better life. Slash and burn agricultural development leaves permanent scars on the Earth. [GUATEMALA]

There is not adequate availability, or sufficient distribution methods, to utilize natural fertilizers on a widespread commercial scale; therefore, a large conversion to "natural" farming systems would reduce productivity significantly. This does not mean that organic farming cannot be successful. In areas such as fruit, vegetable and herb production, organic farming has been more successful than with commodity-driven products. Organic farming should be supported where it is effective, but its limitations to feed a growing world must be realized.

Humans are only one of an estimated 50 to 100 million species that the earth supports. However, we utilize huge amounts of resources and disproportionately affect the availability of these resources. If the human population continues to increase at the current rate, it is estimated that more than half the world's land-based resources will be consumed for human use. Resources in less developed countries (where most of the population growth will occur) are more likely to be depleted at a faster rate. This will include bringing marginal land into production for food while destroying ecosystems in the process. We need a global risk assessment to determine the value of maintaining these biodiverse habitats and to promote the proper role for various farming methods, including high-yield food production systems on the most suitable acreage.

Commercial fishing has gone unchecked in a number of areas throughout the world. Marine biologists have reported that oceanic fisheries are being fished beyond capacity. Here, a boat returns with a day's catch in Malaysia.

Water is a necessity in our daily lives. Here, a young woman collects water in the below-zero early morning temperatures. She must carry the water several miles back to the village where she lives. [CHINA]

(ABOVE) In the next decade, it is estimated that India's population will grow at a rate that will surpass China's.
(OPPOSITE) Torching of forestland has been a common practice in many parts of the world. [BRAZIL]

ENVIRONMENTAL PRESSURES

In the 1980's, a series of news stories described the backlit Amazon jungle being torched for new cropland and grazing areas. During that decade, 175 million acres of Latin America's forests were logged or burned while another 175 million acres were destroyed in Africa and Asia. Currently, less than a quarter of the world's original forest remains. Some estimate that every week one million acres of forestland disappears, and that the rate of deforestation has doubled over the past decade. The consequences of this are widespread, from impact on climatic regulation, to the elimination of habitat for animals. Much of this clearing occurs on hillsides that lose five hundred times more topsoil in a year than if the trees remained in place. A huge portion of the 26 billion tons of soil blown or washed away every year worldwide is largely a result of deforestation.

Over the last 20 years, some estimates show that the world lost enough soil to cover the entire United States!

Although tropical forests account for only six percent of the world's land surface, they are home to about half of all known species on earth. This is the most concentrated biodiversity in the world. These forests often have a higher value when left standing than they do when they are cut. Forests provide climate and water regulation, erosion control, sediment retention, nutrient recycling, genetic material, medicinal resources and cultural benefits. However, these benefits have little meaning if local people have no alternatives for food and other items such as wood for cooking and heating. Therefore, the economic value of these resources must filter back to local communities or they will have little choice but to continue to consume these assets for their own survival.

(TOP AND MIDDLE) Large scale logging operations with no long-term environmental impact assessment will ultimately chip away at habitat critical to the survival of a number of species. [UNITED STATES]

(BOTTOM) Mountain slopes in Uganda, which were once covered with dense vegetation, have been cleared for small patches of farming, destroying prime habitat for the highly endangered mountain gorillas and other species.

The North American temperate rainforest is one of the most productive ecosystems on earth. It is home to many familiar species such as the brown bear and bald eagle. Amazingly, our temperate rainforests have been depleted at a faster rate than some of their tropical counterparts. Clear-cut logging techniques, erosion, and sediment buildup in watersheds have had significant negative impact on salmon populations. Brown bears, black bears, bald eagles and other species depend heavily on a healthy salmon population for their survival. The combination of the depletion of natural habitat, alterations to original waterways, and over-fishing has put pressure on animals throughout the United States and Canada.

Forests are perhaps the most visible resource suffering from human activities such as logging and agricultural development. However, about half the world's wetlands have been lost in the past 100 years and well over half the coral reefs have been damaged by human activity. Today's fishing fleets deplete the ocean's wealth at an unsustainable rate, and increased use of freshwater and groundwater is being consumed at an alarming level. A large part of the problem, in many of these cases, particularly forest depletion and water consumption, is that the true value of these resources is not

(CONTINUES ON PAGE 40)

Some areas of the northwest United States lack coherent long-term policies for the preservation of threatened animal, bird and fish species. Fish resources are facing increasing pressure in these areas. Birds like the bald eagle, depend on salmon to survive.

(LEFT) Forest products are used for a number of local needs. As ecosystems within these forests are destroyed and our biodiversity reduced, we slowly eliminate the opportunity to use nature's science tomorrow. [VIETNAM]

(RIGHT) In many developing countries, irrigation systems are not practical or affordable. However, water is still necessary for successful crop production. [VIETNAM]

An American farmer with modern equipment, in just a few weeks' time, produces enough crops to feed 140 people for a year.

In South Africa, a young girl utilizing primitive agricultural practices, works for months just to help feed her immediate family.

recognized at the "retail" level. Governments subsidize logging activities, water use and, in many cases, agricultural production where it is not a viable activity without economic rationalization. This allows for the consumption of resources at an unnatural and unrealistic rate.

The natural value the earth provides mankind is amazing. Left on its own, the earth provides us with cycles which rejuvenate soils, forests and grasslands, along with clean water and clean air. The more intact the earth remains, or the healthier the planet is in terms of its biological diversity, the more the earth can provide. As we chip away at the planet's resources, we chip away at our own opportunities. As we diminish the available diversity and turn vast unspoiled areas into isolated and unconnected corridors, we create islands of diversity. Some of these islands lose their value as they become disconnected with other species and the interaction they provide. A further impact of this isolation is limited gene pools. Mountain gorillas, cheetahs and tigers are prime examples of species in decline as a result of reduced gene pools. To preserve the necessary habitat to avoid the decline of a number of threatened species, our future policies must encourage more responsible use of our existing resource base. These policies must include food production systems that reduce the need to encroach on vast areas of unspoiled habitat.

Small agricultural plots cut into sides of mountains and through valleys, slowly eroding the continuity of large established forests. This fractionalization threatens many species by reducing suitable habitat and decreasing the genetic diversity of the species. [CHINA]

BIODIVERSITY AND THE FUTURE

Biodiversity supplies a composite of genetic information, provides support for millions of species, is the basis for medicines and pharmaceuticals, and contributes to a network that enhances our food production. There are thousands of lessons to be learned by studying these different forms of nature. For example, the current estimated value of plant-based drugs exceeds 50 billion dollars worldwide. One out of every four drug-related items on the store shelf is derived from a living organism, a product of biodiversity. There may be no limit to the commercial value of what nature can provide. However, when these systems are destroyed, or even disrupted, this wealth of potential benefits shrinks.

The integrity of a fragile ecosystem can be affected by the smallest disruption. Although there are a number of activities that affect these systems, the physical destruction of natural habitat accounts for almost 75 percent of the endangerment of existing species. Almost all deforestation in developing countries is a result of logging or agricultural settlement. The common technique known as slash and burn is responsible for large amounts of forest and jungle destruction.

Land reclamation for incremental agricultural production in established monoculture areas has considerably less impact on the environment than clearing of virgin tropical forests. [UNITED STATES]

Subsistent farmers destroy plots of forest to produce one or two crops per year, usually rice or corn. After a few years they must move to a new area due to low soil fertility. It is often presumed that because of their dense and diverse growth, rainforests have rich soil. In fact, the opposite is often true. In many cases the forest covers an area of poor soil with low nutrient content. The available nutrients are primarily a result of the decay of vegetation and cover and are not found in the composition of the soil itself. The decay and recycling of this vegetation is what helps maintain soil quality. Once cut and removed, unless replaced with commercial fertilizer (rarely used due to availability, cost and distribution issues), the ground becomes less productive. This lack of durability causes new forest to be cleared on an annual basis. As the forest canopy is depleted, heavy rains wash away the nutrients and topsoil which exist. This further reduces the productivity of the land and adds large deposits of sediment to the surrounding watersheds. Sources of food and protection for wildlife are also destroyed as this cycle is repeated.

Because this activity occurs in areas where there are high concentrations of biodiverse habitats, it receives worldwide attention from groups concerned with the results of these practices. Although the United States does not have the intense concentration of species in narrowly defined areas as in some countries,

Pesticide regulation is essentially non-existent in many countries. Pesticides that are banned in the United States continue to be used in other parts of the world. [VIETNAM]

the U.S. is perhaps one of the richest nations when it comes to total number of biodiverse plant and animal species. A joint project commissioned by The Nature Conservancy and the Association for Biodiversity Information reports that approximately 200,000 of the currently 1.75 million species which have been formally listed can be found in the United States. From the West Coast of the U.S. to the East Coast, a variety of species can be located which provide representation of the world's major ecological communities. These ecological areas are as diverse as the San Francisco Bay and the Florida everglades. They include deserts, temperate rainforests, mountains, rivers, swamps, marine ecosystems, meadows, grasslands and other variations of nature's wonders.

The fascinating aspect of the abundance of this biodiversity is that it exists in a country which feeds millions of people worldwide. The United States is better situated to provide food through the use of efficient, high production agricultural practices than any other country in the world. What is more amazing is that the U.S. has the ability to significantly increase its agricultural production with essentially no impact on these 200,000 species. Due to recent farm policies, the United States now has about

Agricultural production in many parts of the world lacks the infrastructure, technology and equipment available to U.S. farmers.

30 million acres of idle land that historically produced crops. Depending on our priorities, the American farmer could supply a large portion of the growing food demands through previously established acreage. Depending on yields and application of improved conservation techniques, this acreage could provide about a 15 percent increase in output without bringing into production a single new acre of land.

There was a period of agricultural development in the U.S. which caused damage to specific species and robbed habitat from wildlife. One of the most well-documented cases of this is the impact of DDT on bald eagle populations, which occurred when DDT was used as a pesticide in agricultural applications. Some of this damage has been repaired and we learned from these experiences. Today, in the United States, it is extremely rare for wildlife habitat to be destroyed for agricultural crop production. About 17 percent of the displacement of species in this country is the result of urban development, roads, logging, mining and agricultural expansion. Agriculture is a very small part of this percentage. If the amount of farm ground lost each year to development is compared to new acreage put into production, it would likely demonstrate a net loss of prime agricultural land.

The United States' success in preserving a number of these species and habitats is due to laws which regulate land use, coupled with efforts to increase public awareness. Striking a balance between competing interests is sometimes difficult and always politically charged. However, our need to balance different interests has provided initiatives that have reduced our impact on nature. Many challenges lie ahead and there continue to be development efforts in various areas of the United States that seem senseless and detrimental to any conservation minded person. The United States Department of Agriculture reported that nationally nearly 16 million acres of forest, cropland and open space were converted to urban and other uses from 1992 to 1997. The average rate for those five years, 3.2 million acres per year, is more than twice the rate of 1.4 million acres a year recorded for the previous decade from 1982 to 1992. At this rate, urban development is a greater threat to habitat destruction in the United States than is agricultural development.

One point illustrated by successful preservation in the U.S., is the way high production farming systems can co-exist with a large variety of biodiversity. With a better understanding of our biological diversity, a broader appreciation of its value, and a balanced approach, the U.S. is a prime example of how a country can feed the world and preserve its natural resources.

Regardless of whether the battle for preservation is in the United States or countries struggling to increase their GDP (gross domestic product), proposed solutions will not be effective if dealt with in isolation. Our efforts will also fail if richer nations think they can establish the rules for poorer nations. We are all guilty of misdeeds. The goal must be to improve on what we have done in the past and learn from our mistakes, not repeat them.

The U.S. currently idles a significant amount of land that previously produced crops. By combining proper conservation improvements on this acreage along with conservation tillage techniques, a large portion of this land is a better choice for food production than the clearing of virgin jungles or forest land elsewhere in the world.

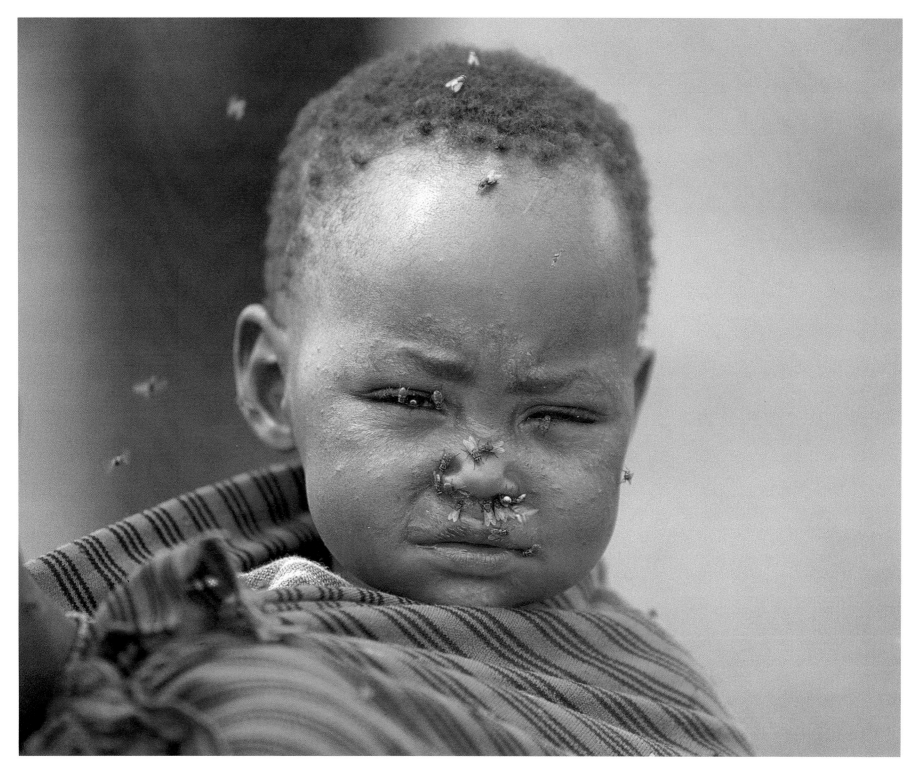

In Tanzania, people in remote villages are concerned with survival, not long-term conservation goals.

Half a world away, this Peruvian girl faces the same challenges to survive.

LONG-TERM CONSEQUENCES

Internal waterways become a way to move grain from one point to another, affecting aquatic life and causing increased river bank erosion. [VIETNAM]

As rural populations migrate to urban areas, more pressure is concentrated on resources in the surrounding area. [MALAYSIA]

Meeting basic needs is a fundamental restriction to achieving sustainable development. Short-term gain, or even survival, often outweigh concerns about long-term damage. Communities in rural areas are forced to exploit local resources as a way of existence. Their immediate needs rule out consideration of future consequences as a result of their behavior. It is not enough to simply explain to people the need to act responsibly. Local economies must be able to support themselves. People must have access to food at a reasonable cost, individual property rights must be enforced equitably, education must be available, and adequate compensation for natural resources must be established. These are complex problems and no single solution will provide the answer.

As this scenario plays out in different parts of the world, countries such as the United States accelerate the problem by reducing food production through various government programs. Every year the U.S. government spends billions of dollars for the purpose of idling fertile cropland. At the same time, countless developing nations subsidize intense production on fragile and marginal soils. Production numbers demonstrate that when the U.S. reduces agricultural output, other countries increase acreage to fill the void. This acreage often comes directly from virgin forests that will never be replaced. Sometimes it is marginal ground which requires more acreage to compensate for lower yields. As this land is developed and agricultural production pushes further and further into new territories, infrastructure development follows. As is the case in many countries, once undisturbed waterways are now being viewed as commercial "highways" to move crops to river ports. All of this activity degrades the habitats and resource base and has a lasting negative impact on the species within the affected area.

IN THE 1980's

U.S. PRODUCTION
DOWN
37 MILLION

Setasides cut U.S. plantings nearly 37 million acres in the 1980's

FOREIGN PRODUCTION
UP
41 MILLION

Foreign farmers took up the slack

When demand for feed grains began to soften in the early 1980's, the U.S. and the rest of the world parted company on strategy. The U.S. reduced planting by 37 million acres and the rest of the world expanded crop production by 41 million acres, roughly a 1-for-1 replacement. This formula held true throughout the decade. What the U.S. took out of production was picked up by growers in competing nations, often at the expense of wildlife habitat.

(DATA SUPPLIED BY ILLINOIS CORN GROWERS ASSOCIATION)

We cannot expect future generations to compensate for our mistakes. Even if technology keeps pace with the demand for food, it cannot replace ecosystems once they have been destroyed, nor is it likely it can regenerate species once they have become extinct. With respect to forests, simply replanting trees does not replace the previous ecosystems nature originally created. Agriculture is not endlessly elastic either. As non-agricultural development encroaches on prime farmland and permanently reduces the ultimate productive capacity of American agriculture, we are on a collision course. Just as the jungles of the Amazon provide international benefits, so does prime productive farmland throughout the Midwest. Therefore, the integration of these resources should be merged into policies that help sustain them on a global basis.

Agriculture throughout the world is a significant aspect of rural life. Solutions for preserving our natural resources on a global basis will require sensitivity to local needs and cultures. [VIETNAM]

CONCLUSION

There is no profession that depends more on the earth and her natural resources than farming, nor is there another industry more vital to human survival than agriculture. Therefore, our existence depends on achieving a balance between agricultural and biological resources. At the same time, high production agriculture must be part of the equation in meeting our future food demands. The policies that determine both the distribution and the use of our natural resources will also affect the long-term sustainability of our capacity to meet these future needs. The failure to properly implement these policies will mean the degradation of two of the most critical resources our world has today, prime agricultural land and wildlife habitats.

Our survival depends on our ability to constantly develop and adapt varieties of plants that overcome disease and improve yields to feed our expanding population. This ability comes from the world's supply of diverse plants and genetic material. It is important that we recognize the value of high-yield agriculture in the effort to maintain this diversity. Our failure to do so will accelerate the demise of biological resources in tropical jungles, wetlands, forests and deserts. This loss will mean foregone opportunities for all of humanity. Agricultural and environmental interests must merge their goals into common achievements. This will not happen unless both groups recognize the value of the contribution each makes to our future. We have the means to use agriculture to our advantage, and we can develop a sustainable model to help maintain biodiversity. The question remains: Do we have the will and the commitment?

The following pages illustrate the many species which depend on a healthy and diverse habitat for survival. Current high yield agricultural production has helped to preserve some of this habitat through increased efficiency, reducing the need on a global basis to bring new acreage into production. However, many of the animals pictured within this book are experiencing extreme pressures on their habitat. With our current policies and priorities, some of these species will not survive.

NORTH AMERICA

From the northern areas of Canada to the southern tip of Mexico, nearly every ecosystem can be found on the North American continent. The diversity ranges from tropical dry forest on the Yucatan Peninsula to the largest temperate rainforest in the world spanning from Northern California to Alaska. It also includes the most complex freshwater wetland system in the world, the Everglades, and one of the largest deserts, the Chihuahuan Desert. The range of landscapes and ecosystems allows for an equally impressive diversity in flora and fauna, much of which is threatened by man.

In the Everglades, the encroachment of sugar cane production and urban sprawl have contributed to the reduction of Florida panthers to less than 50. In areas of Mexico, slash and burn agriculture erodes the last remaining jaguar habitat on this continent. At the opposite end of the North American continent, as far north as the 50th parallel, polar bear research shows that pollution in other parts of the world affects this threatened species.

Not unlike other parts of the world, North America faces a number of environmental challenges. Many of these threats stem from the needs of a technologically advanced society. As a result, this region's resources are pushed to the edge by man's creations rather than by the pressures of simple survival. An issue, such as allocation of water resources, becomes increasingly controversial because of the variety of demands for usage, not because it is difficult to access for daily needs. In North America, irrigation systems pump vast amounts of water to provide abundant crops that are needed to feed people throughout the world. Simultaneously, conservationists fight to preserve water in areas critical to migratory habitats, and cities demand yet even more of this finite resource to meet the needs of urban expansion. These issues differ greatly from those of populations struggling to meet basic needs. It is ironic that such an advanced society, with great wealth and cutting edge technology, has not provided more world leadership in terms of preserving natural resources. In some instances, good leadership has prevailed, but there are also examples where societal advancements have applied more pressure in certain areas of this continent's resource base.

In the United States a broad range of economic and environmental issues are debated, varying from the impact of Genetically Modified Organisms (GMO) to the timber management policies of the U.S. Forestry Service. In Canada, balancing the economic returns from commercial fishing and logging industries competes with maintaining the cultural traditions of Native Indian groups. In Mexico, the recent decision to forego a large industrial complex in the Vizcaino Biosphere Reserve signaled a new commitment to conservation, placing the value of preserving natural resources on an equal level with economic development.

This action by Mexico is significant. Canada and the United States have long been world leaders in legislative initiatives that address environmental and conservation issues. Legislation is not enough; the attitude and spirit of a society also play an important role in the long term ability to achieve goals. Environmental regulation has been a contentious issue in some parts of the United States and Canada. However, there are a number of success stories as a result of the overall commitment to work towards preservation of resources and species. While the debate will continue regarding the reasonable limits of these legislative and regulatory efforts, past achievements have clearly prevented resource depletion in a number of situations.

As you view the photographs on the following pages, imagine a world without these animals and habitats. Envision an environment without the diversity of the Grand Canyon or the Canadian Rockies and all of the species which naturally exist in these habitats. Environmentalism isn't a movement; it is an appreciation of nature and a recognition that humans and animals alike need clean air, pure water and adequate food. Nature, with its finely tuned system of checks and balances, works well; it is man's intervention that causes concern.

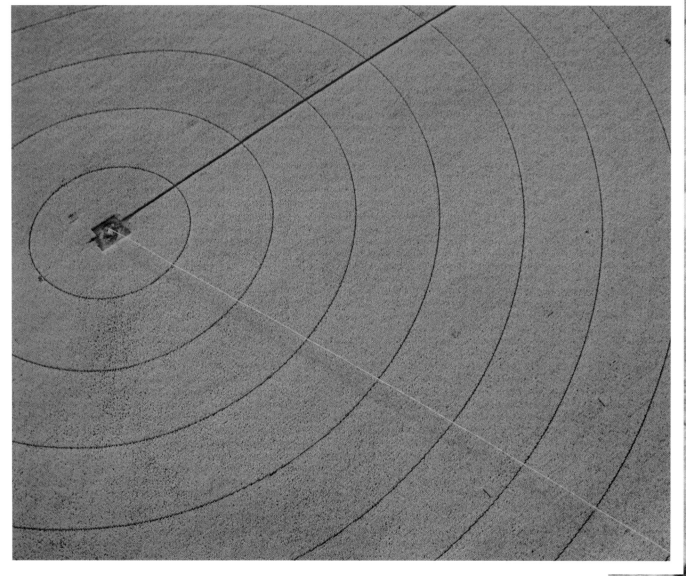

About 15% of the world's cultivated land is irrigated and accounts for almost 40% of the global food harvest. Irrigation is a critical component in maintaining adequate and reliable food production. In some areas, however, over-irrigation has led to total crop failure through salinization. It is estimated that almost 25 million acres are currently lost every year worldwide as a result of poor soil management.

In 1995, over 18 million acres were enrolled into the Conservation Reserve Program. The following year, the United States exported almost $60 billion worth of agricultural products to help meet world food demand. Today over 33 million acres of land previously used for agricultural production lay idle in the U.S., while elsewhere valuable ecosystems are destroyed to develop new cropland. Estimates indicate that by the year 2023 the world population will exceed eight billion people, providing the impetus to develop worldwide sustainable agricultural practices. High yield agriculture on appropriate land, coupled with conservation measures and new technology, is the most sustainable agricultural system yet developed.

Agricultural fields provide food, cover, and nesting material for many birds and animals. No-till and minimum tillage systems leave more residue in tact and more old crop is available to resident species as well as migratory birds. (LEFT, ABOVE) A white-tailed deer bounds across a no-till corn field. (LEFT, BELOW) A coyote takes cover in a no-till field. (RIGHT) A pheasant searches for food in a newly planted corn field.

As the sun set on the 20th century, a new awareness was dawning on the need for highly efficient and conservation-driven agricultural practices.

The U.S. boasts 15,500 different types of flowering plants.
However, about one-third of them are imperiled due to destruction of habitat by humans.

Estuaries are unequalled in their value. They are among the most productive natural systems on Earth, producing more food per acre than the richest Midwest farmland.

Almost 45% of Canada's land area is forested. At least 140,000 species rely on these forests for habitat. At present, an acre of old-growth forest (containing trees which are at least 250 years old) is clear cut every 66 seconds.

*Rivers, lakes and streams account for less than 1% of the Earth's surface;
however, 12% of the world's known animal species exist in these ecosystems.*

Worldwide, the U.S. ranks first in freshwater diversity through its variety of crayfish, mussels and snail species. Global research, however, indicates that 51% of freshwater species are in decline.

The marbled godwit (ABOVE AND OPPOSITE) is one of 49 species of shorebirds that migrate through North America. Conservation initiatives between the U.S. and Mexico have made habitat restoration an urgent priority.

In 1782, the bald eagle (PAGES 70–77) became the national symbol of the United States. At that time population estimates ranged from 100,000 to 250,000. But, 180 years later, only 417 nesting pairs were found in the lower 48 states. Eagle populations in the 19th and 20th centuries were devastated as a result of encroachment on habitat, loss of food sources, and hunting.

In 1940, Congress passed the Bald Eagle Protection Act, which prohibited killing or selling bald eagles. This Act helped raise public awareness of the birds and aided in stabilizing their numbers.

Eagles' primary habitats are quiet coastal areas, rivers, or lakeshores. Expansive urban development in these areas continues to pose a threat to these birds.

Bald eagles can live up to 36 years in the wild and mate for life. Although their range can cover great distances, they normally return to nest within 100 miles of where they were originally raised.

Shortly after World War II, the commercial use of DDT and other organochlorine pesticides became widespread. DDT was sprayed extensively along coastal and other wetland areas to control mosquitoes. Eagles ingested DDT by eating contaminated fish and the pesticides caused the shells of the birds' eggs to thin and break during incubation. The EPA banned the use of these pesticides in 1972.

Raptors, both large and small, require expansive territories to support healthy populations. Destruction of these areas by human intervention is directly linked to species decline.

(THIS PAGE) *American kestrel*
(OPPOSITE) *Osprey*

The diet of the osprey (also referred to as the fish hawk) consists — as one might expect — mainly of fish. Human-induced disturbances such as modified waterways, pesticide pollution, and excessive fishing, threaten the osprey, which (like the bald eagle) is still recovering from the effects of DDT.

The cardinal (ABOVE), originally a bird of the Southeast, is now found in most states across the U.S.
The birds' expanded range is linked to the increased availability of food sources.
(OPPOSITE) Northern bobwhite.

Over 70% of the Earth's surface is covered by water, of which only about 1% is suitable for human consumption. Despite its apparent abundance, water is an increasingly valuable resource.

*Enormous ecosystem diversity is found throughout the United States. This ecological wealth lends itself to the term **megadiversity**.*

North America exemplifies the vast variety of life forms within the biosphere.

When this diversity becomes disrupted, ecosystems become less productive, negatively impacting the species which depend on these habitats.

Plants form the basis for the world's food chain. Over 5,000 different flowering plant species are at risk in the United States.

Recent studies indicate that approximately 90% of all logging in British Columbia utilizes the clear-cutting method — the practice of removing every standing tree. In the United States, it is estimated that only 13% of old-growth forests remain. If consumption of this resource continues at the current rate, these forests could disappear within the next 30-40 years.

While some species of woodpecker have adapted well to orchards and shade trees, most require old wood growth for survival. Two species — the ivory-billed and the red-cockaded woodpecker — require large quantities of mature or dying trees. While both birds are protected under the Endangered Species Act, the ivory-billed woodpecker was listed as extinct in 1995.

The birds shown here are (OPPOSITE PAGE) the red-bellied woodpecker, and (THIS PAGE) the downy woodpecker.

(OVERLEAF) There are roughly 1,400 different types of birds in North America. Of these, approximately 150 are listed as endangered or threatened.

(PAGE 98, CLOCKWISE FROM TOP LEFT) White ibis, sandhill crane, white pelican, sandhill crane.

(PAGE 99, CLOCKWISE FROM TOP LEFT) Yellow warbler, pileated woodpecker, red-headed woodpecker.

The red-tailed hawk is the most common of the raptor family. Often seen perched on roadside telephone poles, this species seems to do well in agricultural areas. This is especially true where conservation tillage is practiced, as it helps to insure a constant supply of primary food sources.

The American kestrel competes with other falcons for hunting and nesting space. As these areas grow smaller, competition for daily survival increases.

There are over 18 different species of owls residing in North America. Their habitat requirements are as different as their features. However, they all face the same threat — man.

(RIGHT AND OPPOSITE) Great horned owl.
(BELOW) Snowy owl.

As part of a restoration program, sandhill cranes have been used as surrogate parents for whooping crane eggs.

Whooping cranes have been protected since 1918. Continuing conservation efforts have allowed population numbers to increase from 21 (in 1941), to about 200 today. Researchers have employed a variety of unique measures in order to save this rare species. Recently scientists used an ultralight airplane to teach crane chicks to migrate from protected areas in Canada to a wildlife refuge in Texas.

There are 9,000 species of birds in the world, of which roughly 15% are found in the United States. Identifying the needs of each is essential for insuring biodiversity. (ABOVE, CLOCKWISE FROM TOP LEFT) Eastern meadowlark, wood duck, sandhill crane, cinnamon teal duck. (OPPOSITE) Red-tailed hawk.

(ABOVE AND OPPOSITE) The mountain lion (sometimes called a cougar or puma) is now included on the Endangered Species List. Once roaming throughout North America, this large cat has been hunted and poisoned to the extent that it is no longer found in the eastern United States.

The red fox (ABOVE AND OPPOSITE) has one of the largest ranges of any carnivore. It has learned to adapt to human interference, perhaps better than any other species.

The gray fox (ABOVE), shy in nature, is sensitive to changes in habitat. It prefers secluded woodlands and rocky areas close to marshes, avoiding unnecessary contact with humans. Arctic foxes (OPPOSITE) are in conflict with red foxes as a result of the latter's continuously expanding territory. They now both compete for survival in the Arctic Circle.

Arctic foxes (LEFT) are genetically engineered to endure extremely cold climates. They are relatively tolerant of humans. As scavengers, these foxes often feed on the remains of polar bear kills, thus helping maintain the delicate balance of the Arctic tundra. Unlike arctic foxes, arctic wolves (ABOVE) avoid humans.

(LEFT) *Timber wolf. The largest of the canine group, wolves are fiercely territorial. Same species predation occurs with some regularity, perhaps insuring true survival of the fittest.*

(RIGHT) *Contrary to myths and legends, wolves do not howl at the moon, they howl to each other — as a form of communication. Vocal cues are thought to provide information about territories, pack size, and location.*

Perceiving them as a menace, man proceeded to exterminate wolves in the lower 48 states in the early 20th Century. A program to reintroduce wolves to the United States now supports several populations, from Yellowstone National Park to areas in Minnesota.

The population of the Canada lynx (ABOVE) is currently stable. However, its relative, the Iberian lynx, is not as fortunate — it is one of the 10,800 species listed as threatened or endangered in the World Conservation Union's 2000 Red List report.

The coyote (ABOVE AND OPPOSITE) is an exceptional athlete. The best runner of its species, the coyote has been tracked at speeds of up to 40 miles per hour. It has also been recorded traveling great distances, up to 400 miles.

The coyote's reputation as wily perhaps describes its astounding ability to hunt for food. It has been seen fishing for carp, digging for turtle eggs and following vultures in search of carrion.

Although eliminated from most of its southern range, the American elk still numbers 400,000 strong throughout the Great Plains and western mountain ranges.

Reduction or elimination of natural predators (such as the wolf) allows deer to remain the most abundant of all large game animals in the United States. Deer populations are often controlled through managed hunting programs.

There are twenty-seven different types of whales found in the world's oceans. Historically, some whales have been persecuted to the brink of extinction. Constantly enduring threats such as toxins, noise pollution and exploitative fishing practices, eight of these species are now listed as endangered. (ABOVE AND OPPOSITE) Gray whale.

According to the United States Fish and Wildlife Service, approximately 22,000–28,000 polar bears (PAGES 126–139) exist worldwide. Although they are not in immediate danger of extinction, they face threats common to large predators: human encroachment, illegal hunting and toxic contamination of their food sources.

In October of 2000, the United States and Russia signed an accord for the conservation of polar bear populations shared between the two countries. The agreement, waiting for ratification by the U.S. Senate, will provide long-term joint conservation management programs, which will emphasize population research and coordination of habitat conservation measures.

131

Scientists record weights and measurements, and identify polar bears by using tattoos and radio collars. This essential information allows scientists to track the growth and development of bears as well as population and movement statistics.

The longest running and most comprehensive study on polar bear populations has been conducted in Canada. For the last twenty years researchers have studied the habits of polar bears in the Churchill, Manitoba region. Through this study, test results of fat samples have found increasing amounts of PCB's and other hazardous toxins.

Although now extinct in 7 of the 48 contiguous states, population numbers of American black bears (THIS PAGE AND OPPOSITE) have not significantly decreased since early Europeans first arrived in North America.

As with so many other species, human conflict remains the primary source of stress for bear populations. Bears become habituated (conditioned to humans). This is well illustrated by their habit of feeding at public garbage dumps, which supply the bears with vast amounts of unnatural foods. This type of behavior disrupts the bears' normal life cycle, increases illness, causes premature death, and can also lead to the extermination of problem bears.

The brown bear (PAGES 142-147) has perfected the art of salmon fishing. Scouting out productive spawning spots, brown bears have been known to stand mid-stream and wait for fish to jump into their gaping jaws. These ideal fishing spots, however, have become few. Sedimentation from logging, devastation from pollutants and the impact of altered waterways have all affected these important fishing locations.

Man and bear have been in conflict for thousands of years. Both are direct competitors for space and resources around the world. Man, however, being excellent at exploiting resources and less tolerant of nature, continues to challenge the sustainability of this species.

SOUTH AMERICA

The South American continent includes the most biodiverse ecosystems in the world. Certain areas of Brazil and Peru have the highest concentrations of diverse species that have ever been recorded. The Amazon, in Brazil, is the earth's largest tropical rainforest. Its 2.5 million square miles include 500 different species of mammals, over 400 species of reptiles and in excess of 30 percent of the world's birds. The Amazon is one of this planet's most poignant examples of the threat to millions of undiscovered species by the expansion of commercial and subsistent agricultural growth.

Peru is home to the Manu National Park, which is a smaller version of the Amazon Basin, with more than 800 bird species and a high concentration of monkeys, bats and amphibians. Manu, like the Amazon, holds many undiscovered plants and animals. It is estimated that the area contains around 500,000 species of arthropod and has a number of species which are globally threatened, including the jaguar.

More importantly, it is in these areas that man could very possibly find cures for cancer, AIDS and other medical problems. History has proven that nature has many ways of providing solutions that are beyond man's ability to create. The World Health Organization has estimated that 80 percent of the world's population depends on plant and animal based remedies for medically related treatments. The rainforest offers literally millions of opportunities; but these opportunities disappear as fast as we destroy the very forest we need.

In addition to areas such as the Amazon and Manu, within the borders of Brazil and Paraguay lies the largest fresh-water wetland system in the world, the Pantanal. The Pantanal covers approximately 96,000 square miles and is an area larger than the state of Oregon. It is home to a large variety of birds, mammals and the giant otter, one of the most endangered animals in the world.

A majority of the Pantanal is found in two states in Brazil; the Mato Grosso do Sul and the Mato Grosso. These areas have seen large portions of virgin jungle transformed into areas for cattle grazing. Now, some of the grazing areas are being converted to crop production. Without intervention, this cycle puts the preservation of these unique and irreplaceable resources on a collision course with future agricultural demands.

There have been creative efforts to address these issues. One method has been to provide suitable farmland to indigenous communities in exchange for tropical forest in areas where natives have habitually applied slash and burn methods in order to plant corn and beans. The Nature Conservancy was instrumental in helping to achieve such a "land swap" in the Sierra de las Minas Bio-sphere Reserve in Guatemala. This concept, exchanging farmland for wilderness, will preserve precious habitat. Another approach that has been developed is a "debt for nature swap". Such a swap in Brazil has led to the protection of the Grande Sertão Veredas National Park. The Nature Conservancy purchased Brazilian government debt in the secondary market and exchanged it for an agreement that supports conservation efforts for the life of the original debt. In April of 1992 World Wildlife Fund in Japan and the Dai-Ichi Kangyo Bank announced a one million-dollar debt-for-nature swap which would contribute to conservation of the Galapagos Islands in Ecuador. Creative concepts like these must continue to be developed and implemented to protect our natural resources.

There are many other important ecological areas in South America. From Patagonia to the shorelines of Chile, there are a number of unique ecosystems and an impressive variety of animals. The indigenous tribes of South America have incorporated these resources into their cultures for thousands of years. The question is whether sustainable practices will allow for future generations to benefit from these same resources. The following photographs provide visual images of what is at stake.

There are approximately 30 different types of parrots, macaws and parakeets indigenous to the South American continent — almost all of which are listed as endangered as a result of human activity. (ABOVE) Blue and yellow macaw.

Due to insatiable demand, illegal "cage-bird" trade has reduced wild populations of the hyacinth macaw (ABOVE) from 50,000 to approximately 3,000.

Despite multi-national conservation efforts, wild macaw populations face an uncertain future as a result of illegal bird trade and deforestation of their natural habitat. (ABOVE AND OPPOSITE) Scarlet macaw.

Destruction of habitat has accelerated world-wide. As a result, 12% of all bird species are threatened by global extinction.

(THIS PAGE) *Lesser Kiskadee flycatcher.*
(OPPOSITE) *Roadside hawk.*

(OVERLEAF)
PAGE 158 (TOP) *Chestnut-eared aracari.*
    (BOTTOM) *Toco toucan.*
PAGE 159 (TOP) *Keel-billed toucan.*
    (BOTTOM) *Red-breasted toucan.*

Most often associated with the icy cold, the majority of *penguins* are actually warm weather birds. Six species are native to the coastal areas of South America, with one — the Peruvian penguin — being listed as endangered.

Studies indicate that we have already lost more than 60% of the earth's primary tropical rainforests. Dramatic losses such as this seriously imperil predatory species like the black hawk eagle (ABOVE) and the black-and-white hawk eagle (OPPOSITE).

Species such as the yellow-billed cardinal (LEFT) and the green kingfisher (OPPOSITE) depend on the diversity which exists in tropical forests, wetlands and marshes.

A spectacular component of wetland biodiversity is the shorebird migration. Millions of individuals of some 40 species travel from their breeding grounds in North America to the highly productive wetlands in South America, where they find an abundance of food. (ABOVE) *Peruvian pelican.* (OPPOSITE) *Flamingo.*

(THIS PAGE)
Great egret.

(OPPOSITE)
Blue and white swallow.

168

(ABOVE) Snowy egret. (OPPOSITE) Tiger heron. Habitat loss and degradation are the most pervasive threats to avian life, affecting 89% of all threatened birds. For example, 40% of the 215 species of indigenous birds in the Brazilian Atlantic Forest are threatened.

(LEFT) *Plush crested jay.*
(BELOW) *Ringed kingfisher.*

(BELOW) Great white egret.
(RIGHT) Guira cuckoo.

In the 1960's, an estimated 15,000 jaguars (PAGES 174-178) were slaughtered in the Amazon area of Brazil alone.
The jaguar is internationally recognized as a species at risk. The decline of the jaguar is a result of the same factors affecting other
large cats: persecution as a predator, habitat loss and commercial fur hunting.

The encroachment into South America's tropical forests has been devastating. Of the original forests, as little as 3% remains today.

Estimates indicate that 45% of the world's cropland has been affected by land degradation, including soil erosion, nutrient deficiency, salinity and chemical build-up. Over-grazing for cattle production poses a similar threat to the sustainability of the soil. Developed countries, utilizing high-yield farming procedures, have the least degraded soil.

Freshwater rivers are a significant resource required by many species for survival. Iguazu Falls is a special basin where the Parana and Iguapa Rivers combine. Other rivers in Brazil are also significant. The Amazon River alone accounts for more than 20% of the world's renewable fresh water. Many of these rivers are now used as water highways to transport commercial and industrial products. This increased traffic negatively impacts the ecosystems and the species which rely on them for survival.

Common squirrel monkeys are indigenous to the northern region of South America.
Prior to protective conservation efforts, these primates were extensively exported for sale as pets and for biomedical research projects.

There are 17 species of iguana listed as threatened or endangered.
In addition to conflict with humans, the introduction of invasive foreign species has had a negative effect on native populations.

The Paraguayan caiman (ABOVE AND OPPOSITE) was once heavily poached.
An estimated 1,000,000 skins were obtained illegally in the 1970's and 1980's.

The Amazonian canopy is roughly nine times the size of Texas. This tree-top environment is home to the three-toed sloth (ABOVE AND OPPOSITE) and perhaps, as scientists estimate, half the world's species.

The ring-tailed lemur (ABOVE), along with other lemurs and marmosets, are imperiled due to hunting and loss of habitat. Almost one-third of all lemur species that once existed are now extinct.

*The golden lion tamarin (*ABOVE*) is indigenous to the primary low-land forests of Brazil.*
Conversion of land to pasture cattle has caused the tamarin to become one of the world's most endangered species.

Many species are vital to the survival of others as exemplified in the relationship between the Caramujeiro hawk and the snails (ABOVE) on which it feeds. A decline in the snail population directly threatens the hawk and the survival of other species. Interrelationships such as these are rarely considered or recognized.

The need to better identify the importance of each species is imperative to the sustainability of all ecosystems. Like the bee and the turtle (ABOVE) every individual is an essential part of the delicate balance of nature.

The giant otter (ABOVE AND OPPOSITE) is the rarest mammal in the Amazon. Illegal exploitation of the otter for the fur trade has resulted in this animal virtually disappearing from Argentina, Uruguay, and southeastern Brazil.

ASIA

Asia is the largest continent in the world, in both population and size. It covers almost one third of the world's land area and reaches from the Arctic in the North to the tropics in the South. Asia is a geography course unveiled; it is home to the highest and lowest places on earth, the largest rivers, greatest deserts and thickest forests and jungles. Therefore, with both the intense natural diversity and the huge growing population, parts of Asia are a case study of man in conflict with nature.

With millions of people living along the continent's rivers, river valleys and deltas, watershed protection is scarce. The heavily farmed delta areas cause sediment to be washed into the river systems. Inefficient irrigation methods consume unnecessary quantities of water while larger tributaries are used heavily for transportation. About three-fifths of the population of Asia makes a living through agriculture, putting immense pressure on land-based resources. As demand for food increases, a large number of Asia's diverse ecosystems could be used for additional agricultural production or other applications. As this occurs, available habitat for animal and bird species will disappear.

There are, however, areas where success has been achieved. A recent agricultural experiment in China, one of the largest ever undertaken, drastically reduced crop loss by simply planting different varieties of rice in the same field. Normally, large amounts of chemical fungicide applications are required to reduce the damage to rice crops from a disease known as "rice blast." This experiment was so successful that within two years farmers have abandoned the use of chemical fungicides and have still maintained yields. This success reduces the need to expand production into new acreage and reduces chemical fungicide use. It also provides the impetus to determine if greater diversity could achieve similar results in other monoculture production applications.

Additional progress is necessary to deal successfully with Asia's 49 countries. China has the world's largest population while India has one of the world's fastest growing populations. There are also a number of islands scattered throughout Asia, such as Indonesia, the Philippines, Malaysia and Japan. The southern islands rival some of their counterparts in South and Central America for species and plant diversity. Asia's animal species vary from arctic foxes in the north to orangutans in the south and the plant diversity ranges from rubber trees to spruce and fir. A continent so rich in variety provides ample opportunity for resource abuse. Among other problems, authorities must deal with illegal logging and poaching. Because Asia is home to some of the most endangered animals on earth, this activity has significant consequences. The panda, snow leopard and several subspecies of tigers are the best recognized animals under threat in Asia. These species are threatened for a number of reasons, though loss of habitat is the greatest single cause.

For this reason, the forests in China's Xishuangbanna Prefecture are recognized as a priority conservation area. These forests are China's largest tropical forests, but already half of them have been lost to rubber and tea plantations. Slash and burn agriculture has also added to the toll, accounting for the destruction of about 25,000 acres. This "shifting agriculture" has contributed heavily to soil erosion, turning once clear rivers into rivers of mud. The World Wildlife Fund has made progress in addressing the destruction of these forests through developing and promoting ecologically benign methods of producing food and fuel. New agriforestry methods are being taught and integrated with community-based forest management programs; some progress in dealing with the long-term health of these forests has been achieved.

China has also launched a long-term conservation effort to preserve the virgin forests along the upper Yangtze River, the upper and middle Yellow River and the Inner Mongolia region. A special fund valued at over $11 billion has been established to insure the success of this undertaking. Simultaneously, China launched a logging ban in many state-owned forests. These and other projects mark a new threshold for conservation in China.

The future choice will be to preserve this habitat by using more suitable land to produce food, or to watch the destruction of irreplaceable ecosystems and species. The choice to preserve, however, will require bold leadership and unprecedented cooperation.

The panda (ABOVE AND OPPOSITE), a popular symbol of conservation, is China's flagship species. It is believed that currently as few as 1,000 individuals are left in the wild. Destruction of the panda's habitat has left them virtually stranded in "pockets". Fragmentation has severely limited the pandas' flexibility to find adequate food supplies and has also led to isolated populations, which pose the common threats associated with a reduced gene pool.

The primary threat to the survival of the panda is habitat destruction due to logging and farming. The Chinese government recently banned logging in some forests in an effort to provide protection for the panda.

(LEFT AND RIGHT) *Japan alone consumes four times more fish each year than the world average. Japan has now become the world's largest importer of fish and shellfish, accounting for one-third of all world imports. Competition for similar food sources — such as fish — continues to create conflict between humans and other species.*

(OPPOSITE, TOP) *Brown bear.*

(OPPOSITE, BOTTOM) *Cormorant.*

(OVERLEAF, LEFT) *Marine fishing generates approximately 1% of the global economy and supports the livelihoods of around 200 million people worldwide. Exploitive fishing practices threaten the sustainability of this industry and the viability of marine ecosystems. It is estimated that overfishing has already depleted 69% of the world's major fish species.*

(OVERLEAF, RIGHT) *Unsustainable fishing practices around the world have created serious problems in oceans, lakes, and streams. Long-line fishing nets are responsible for the destruction of thousands of ocean birds. Industrial pollutants foul fresh lakes and streams while exploitive fishing practices diminish world fish supplies.*

Because bears are regarded as direct competitors for food resources, they are afforded no protection under Japanese law, even within the confines of Japan's National Parks. Non-Governmental Organizations (NGOs) therefore provide information about the dangers of human activities that put man and bear in conflict. In contrast to initiatives implemented in most U.S. National Parks, these signs are often the only education that visitors receive. When a human/bear conflict arises, the bear is usually killed rather than relocated.

(LEFT) *To determine the best policy to protect the bears in Shiretoko National Park, this ranger tracks a bear fitted with a radio transmitter. This information helps rangers determine bear movements and can help prevent conflicts with humans. With limited funds to conduct research, only seven radio collars have been deployed in the entire 94,000 acres of the park. Unfortunately, the lack of financial resources prevents the undertaking of a comprehensive study to provide adequate information on bear populations.*

(RIGHT) *Conservation efforts in many parts of the world are limited in their effect due to lack of resources, weak policy enforcement and poor inter-agency co-operation. In Japan, this constitutes a major impediment in the conservation and management of biodiversity. These rangers, understaffed and provided with minimal support from the government, are the only resource committed to keeping wildlife populations healthy. However, commercial concerns take precedence over conservation efforts, providing a frustrating challenge for those who wish to protect wildlife.*

Hunting and illegal trade in bear parts for oriental medicinal purposes continue, even though the brown bear (ABOVE AND OPPOSITE) is protected under strict regulations of the Convention on International Trade in Endangered Species. Although this international monitoring program was established to control global trade in threatened wildlife and wildlife products, a lack of enforcement and resources hampers its effectiveness.

In Japan, wildlife is afforded little protection when it comes into direct conflict with human interests. The brown bear found in Japan — similar to those found in North America — competes with humans for fishing space among the rivers and streams. In Japan, where bears are considered to have no commercial value, they are often looked upon as a nuisance.

(ABOVE , OPPOSITE AND OVERLEAF) Red fox. The national park system in Japan allows for local jurisdiction to prevail in instances where community or private property falls within the boundaries of the park. This makes the execution of a comprehensive wildlife plan nearly impossible. Competing interests within governmental bureaucracies also cause difficulty in implementing long-term strategies. Without changes in attitudes regarding commercial activity and legislative initiatives for the protection of species, the future for many animals remains uncertain.

In Asia, 60% of the world's population depends on 30% of the land for sustenance. Consequently, the pressure results in conflict between man and species as ecosystems are disrupted or destroyed. This continual degradation threatens many species, from large raptors such as the crested serpent eagle (LEFT) to inconspicuous insects like bees (ABOVE).

(THIS PAGE AND OPPOSITE, LEFT TO RIGHT) Collared scops owls, black-rumped flameback woodpecker, rose-ringed parakeet, Alexandrine parakeet.

(OPPOSITE, LEFT TO RIGHT) Little egret, red-wattled lapwing plover, Indian pond heron. (ABOVE) Common kingfisher.

White-rumped shama (OPPOSITE) and rainbow lorikeet (ABOVE). Many birds, including species found in Asia, face similar threats to their environment. Unfortunately, even in protected areas, illegal logging further reduces available habitat. In addition to habitat loss, in many areas, illegal cage-bird trade compounds pressures on remaining wild populations.

*Forced from lower agricultural areas where farming has expanded, Japanese macaques (*PAGES *221–224), also referred to as snow monkeys, have adapted to life in the cold regions of Japan's boreal forests.*

221

Habitat conversion has resulted in escalating conflicts between the snow monkey and man. As a result, hundreds of these monkeys are captured or shot each year because they are perceived as agricultural pests.

PAGE 225:
Long-tailed macaque monkey.

Despite international restrictions on the sale of primates for pets, illegal trade continues. Lack of government enforcement, corruption and greed are the driving forces behind illegal pet trade, fueling it into a multi-billion dollar-a-year industry. Captured monkeys are subjected to inhumane conditions, which result in many deaths. Even with existing provisions designed to protect endangered species, the trade in these mammals continues to flourish.

Fines averaging U.S. $50,000 are imposed on anyone owning, hunting, or transporting an orangutan (LEFT, BELOW) in Indonesia. Still, despite international protection, the illegal trade practice continues.

(ABOVE) Long-tailed macaque.
(OPPOSITE) Rhesus monkey.

227

Like other large predators, the snow leopard (ABOVE AND OPPOSITE) faces continual shortages of food sources due, in part, to deforestation and loss of habitat. These animals have been nearly exterminated from their native environment as a result of conflicts with domestic livestock and because of their value in the commercial fur trade. New conflict has arisen in this century, as the snow leopard has become a substitute for the tiger in Oriental medicines. Ironically, tighter regulations, which seek to control the use of tiger parts in traditional Chinese medicines, have diverted tiger poaching efforts towards hunting snow leopards for similar traditional uses. This has caused increasing declines among already threatened populations.

(ABOVE) A national park guard uses a makeshift frame to apply a plaster substance for recording paw prints of a tiger. These prints help determine population numbers, territory and behavior patterns.

(OPPOSITE) The sloth bear is listed under Appendix I of CITES, which means it is one of the most threatened species. These bears are not likely found outside protected areas such as national parks and preserves due to fractionalized habitat and poaching.

In 1972, the tiger received a final listing under the Endangered Species Act. Lack of enforcement of trade sanctions has resulted in the continued poaching of tigers for use in oriental medicines. Reports indicate that in South Korea alone, over six tons of tiger bone was imported between 1975 and 1992. (ABOVE) Sumatran tiger. (OPPOSITE) Indochinese tiger.

Indochinese tiger.

Bengal tiger.

Of the eight sub-species of tigers, three have become extinct within the last 60 years. One species, the Chinese tiger (**panthera tigris amoyensis**) went from a population of approximately 4,000 in 1949 to as few as 30–40 individuals in the wild today. There are five sub-species of tigers roaming the remaining forests of Asia and Europe. Populations in the early 1980's were reported around 100,000. As a result of continued persecution, the estimated number of tigers currently living in the wild ranges from 5,000–7,000 individuals. Tragically, it is reported that even if the tiger had no commercial value, its long-term survival would still be threatened by the destruction of its habitat.

(THIS PAGE AND OPPOSITE, TOP) *Siberian tiger.*
(OPPOSITE, BOTTOM) *Bengal tiger.*

236

(ABOVE AND OPPOSITE) Bengal tiger.

As this Bengal tigress moves off into the morning fog in Ranthambhore National Park, her future, along with that of her species, remains uncertain.

AFRICA

Africa is an immense continent with great diversity and, though rich with natural resources such as diamonds, gold and timber, poverty is also pervasive. It is a continent where nations expend resources fighting neighboring countries as their people starve. Yet, there is another part of Africa that makes it a magnet to adventurers. From the Nile River to the Okavango Delta, Africa exhibits incredible beauty.

Africa presents the most prominent examples of how man has lived with nature. Tribes such as the Maasai have co-existed with the greatest of predators. Perhaps it is in this primitive condition that the most important lesson of all can be learned. The indigenous people of Africa have not survived out of fear of nature; they have survived as a result of respecting nature.

In fact, Africa's future lies in the success of harnessing this respect for nature and skillfully using it to protect valuable resources while allowing it to provide economic opportunities. This is an area of the world that must incorporate eco-tourism as part of its mainstream economy. The reason is simple; mining and logging can provide only a minimum of jobs, yet there are huge untapped opportunities for eco-entrepreneurs.

There is only one Serengeti ecosystem, where the plains are home to the greatest animal migration. There is only one Virunga Mountain Range, where the world's only mountain gorillas exist. There is also only one place you can smell the breath of a wild lion and go home to write about it — Africa.

This continent is unique in that it is home to more predators than any other place in the world. Several of these species, such as the painted hunting dog (African wild dog), are the most endangered in the world. Others, such as the cheetah, are highly threatened and continue to face increasing odds against survival as time passes. Sometimes it is difficult to balance conservation efforts to help preserve these animals, since these initiatives conflict with the livelihood of the indigenous tribes or farmers. As cheetahs are pushed further and further to the edge of their natural habitat, they may find cattle or sheep an easier meal than an impala in the wild. These conflicts require creative solutions and cooperation. In South Africa, the Wild Cheetah Management Program has been implemented to capture and relocate problem cheetahs before they are shot by farmers. It is not surprising that with Africa's immense size these challenges occur frequently and under many different conditions.

Africa covers about a fifth of the world's land area with the northern part of Africa just short of the northern 40th parallel. The southern half stretches past the equator almost reaching the southern 40th parallel. The equator essentially bisects this continent. This vast land is home to at least 29 major tribes with many sub-groups scattered throughout. As the result of early colonization, combined with this great diversity of people, it is estimated that over 2,000 languages are spoken throughout Africa.

Although many African tribes have been strongly influenced by the European presence since the 1400's, there are still a number of tribes that incorporate traditional parts of their culture into their lives. The Yoruba of southwestern Nigeria and neighboring Benin and Togo are believed to have formed their kingdom around 850 A.D. The traditional Yoruba religion is centered around a pantheon of deities. "Mande" is a large family of languages spoken by a great number of West African ethnic groups. It also is applied to the people of the geographic areas that these groups occupy. One of the most famous tribes of Africa is the Maasai. The image of a Maasai warrior clutching a spear and wearing the traditional red cloth has become a familiar one. Maasai life revolves entirely around cattle ownership. They believe God entrusted His cattle to them and consequently their wealth is measured by the number of cattle they have acquired. All of these various tribes continue to incorporate their traditional culture in their lives even though the world around them is constantly changing.

Africa is unique in all that it offers. There are areas where commerce thrives and places where cattle graze and crops flourish. But the real Africa is found outside the city limits and away from its fences and farms. This is an area of the world that supports an incredible variety of animals, but it is also facing some of the most difficult challenges. Many Africans have the mind-set and determination to overcome these challenges, but the question remains, does the political leadership have the will? If so, Africa will remain a destination that will always offer special opportunities, no matter how many times you set foot on the continent.

Elephants (PAGES 244–248) are the largest land mammals on earth. This species was driven dangerously close to extinction by European settlers and ivory hunters during the late 1800's. Conservation foresight led to the establishment of the Kruger National Park in 1898, which provided protected areas for endangered species, including the elephant. Even within these areas elephants remain under threat due to illegal trade in ivory and loss of habitat resulting from human population pressures. In South Africa, elephants have been translocated to approximately forty different locations. This concerted conservation effort has allowed the number of elephants in South Africa to grow from 120 (in 1920) to nearly 10,000 animals today.

Two species of rhinoceros are found on the continent of Africa, the black rhino and the white rhino. The invasive practices of man threaten both. The effects of habitat destruction and poaching have dramatically reduced rhino populations. The rhino's horn — highly sought by poachers — is actually made up of thousands of strands of **keratin**, which is the same substance that is found in human fingernails.

The effort to save the white rhino (LEFT AND OPPOSITE) is an example of combined conservation efforts. Protection in the reserves and parks in southern Africa has allowed wild populations to increase slightly. In addition to these protected areas, the American Zoo and Aquarium Association has been successful in supporting re-introduction programs of captive-bred rhinos into the wild. Nevertheless, these animals remain highly endangered.

251

Africa supports only two species of hippo: the pygmy, and the common hippopotamus (ABOVE AND OPPOSITE). Today, the main conservation threat is no longer hunting but loss of habitat. Unsustainable irrigation practices have resulted in rivers drying up at a faster rate, leaving these "river horses" with fewer places to live.

A unique adaptation of the hippo is the ability to lie in the water for most of its life. This allows it to avoid predators and keep its skin moist. Hippos play host to a variety of different species while submerged, as fish graze on the algae that grow on their backs, and young crocodiles, turtles and birds use them as resting platforms. The hippo is an excellent example of how one element in a chain can support a variety of interactions within a single ecosystem.

Water use throughout Africa has been impacted by poor irrigation techniques and increasing demands for agricultural production. Unsustainable practices in arid regions have caused life-sustaining water holes to dry up more quickly. Nyala (LEFT) and vervet monkey (RIGHT).

With more than a quarter of a billion people in Africa denied access to adequate water supplies, tension remains high as man and animals continually compete for a diminishing resource.

OPPOSITE: (TOP AND BOTTOM) **Blue wildebeest.**

(LEFT) Grant's gazelle. (RIGHT) Impala.

(LEFT) *Nyala.* (RIGHT) *Waterbuck.*

Estimates conclude that the human population of Africa is expected to grow to over one billion people by 2025. Facing the challenge of how to meet the needs of a burgeoning population while protecting biodiverse and sensitive ecosystems remains a difficult task. (ABOVE) *Impala.* (OPPOSITE) *Waterbuck.*

(OPPOSITE) Red lechwe. (ABOVE) Steenbok.
(OVERLEAF, RIGHT) Bushbuck.

22 of the approximately 65 species of egrets, herons and bitterns reside in Africa. The intermediate egret (ABOVE) along with the cattle egret have established symbiotic relationships with larger animals of the African plains. These birds feed on insects carried or disturbed by buffaloes, elephants and other migratory animals. (OPPOSITE) Roan antelope.

Africa is home to a spectacular array of avian fauna. Species include the crowned crane (ABOVE), and (OPPOSITE PAGE, CLOCKWISE FROM TOP LEFT) bateleur eagle, white-fronted bee-eater, little bee-eater, and grey hornbill.

Ironically, man's interference with natural habitats has actually benefitted certain species, such as the spur-winged goose (ABOVE). Goose populations have flourished as the result of the construction of dams in farm areas. These man-made structures, along with agricultural production, have provided an ideal habitat and a source of abundant food. The spur-winged goose has prospered so well in some commercial cropland areas that they are now seen as pests.

The species shown above are (CLOCKWISE FROM TOP LEFT):
Lilac breasted roller, fish eagle, black-bellied korhaan, crested barbet.

Each species develops unique adaptations to insure its survival. The yellow-billed stork (ABOVE) has a touch-sensitive bill, which helps it locate food in the murky waters of its habitat. (OPPOSITE) The flightless adaptation found in jackass penguins is a product of more than 100 million years of evolutionary development. What they lack in flying abilities, they possess in swimming skills, which are equivalent to those of dolphins and seals.

*Disease, contamination from domesticated animals, combined with uncontrolled hunting, nearly eliminated the giraffe (PAGES 274–278) from East Africa. Although it is illegal, poaching continues in many African countries. Remaining populations of giraffe have been classified as **conservation dependent**.*

The veld areas, or distinct ecosystems occurring on the African continent, support an enormous variety of ungulates.
(OPPOSITE): Giraffe and Burchell's zebra. (PAGES 279–283): Burchell's zebra.

The zebra community is a tightly knit organization and the animals tend to live in small familial groups. Indiscriminate hunting has left two of the three species of zebra endangered, leaving them to exist mainly in protected areas.

Maintaining healthy ecosystems insures sustainable biodiversity. Understanding the importance of every species, from the dwarf mongoose (ABOVE) to the mite and the dragonfly (OPPOSITE), is paramount to insuring the viability of each inhabitant.

(LEFT) *Side-striped jackal.* (ABOVE) *The painted hunting dog (African wild dog, **Lycaon pictus**) is one of Africa's most endangered species. As in the case of the zebra, each dog has a distinctive pattern to its marbled coat, allowing researchers to identify and track individuals more easily. The wild dog is said to be the world's most efficient mammalian hunter. However, disease transmission from domesticated animals, loss of habitat and lion predation has contributed to continued pressure on this species.*

The lion (PAGES 288–302) has historically been perceived as the king of the beasts and a symbol of majesty. Today, however, the lion is a victim — weakened by the effects of human encroachment. Persecution as a predator, introduction of domestic animals (resulting in disease and habitat fragmentation) and sport hunting have all contributed to the rapid decline of the species. Once found throughout most of Europe, Asia and Africa, today only fragmented populations of lions remain in Africa. Two lion subspecies, the Barbary and the Cape lion, are listed as extinct; a third subspecies, the Asiatic lion, is listed as critically endangered.

In the Kruger National Park (South Africa) the spread of tuberculosis (TB) to lion prides has compounded the strain on already stressed populations. It is speculated that the disease was spread by a single buffalo that encountered infected domestic cattle. In an effort to pinpoint the cause of the TB outbreak among lions, scientists tested buffaloes, the lions' main source of food. Ninety percent of the six hundred buffaloes tested were contaminated with the TB virus. Recontamination through eating infected food is responsible for the death of fifty percent of the resident lion population.

The African lion is extinct in most of the northern section of the African continent.

Though the male lion is attributed with strength and prowess, the female, in fact, does most of the hunting, in addition to raising the cubs.

302

The leopard (PAGES 303–311), *whether perched in a tree or hunting on the ground, remains the master of camouflage, while the distinctive pattern of its coat makes this one of the most beautiful of the large cats. Highly adaptable and widely distributed throughout most of Africa (although exact numbers are unknown), the leopard has not been able to conceal itself from the constant intrusion of man. Intensification of agriculture and elimination of natural prey have caused conflict between farmers and leopards. Fur trade took an estimated 50,000 leopards annually in the mid 1990's. With little place left to hide, the leopard is now protected throughout Africa. However, in certain areas the leopard's range has been drastically reduced by agricultural development.*

A diminished genetic pool has left the cheetah (PAGES *312–325) highly vulnerable. Genetic similarities, as seen in cheetah populations, are believed to have serious implications for the survival of this species. This anomaly has left the cheetah prone to sperm abnormalities, decreased reproductive rates, and increased susceptibility to disease.*

An estimated 60% of wild cheetah cubs are lost to predation, mostly by lions. Those that do survive face a difficult future. Human conflict continues to threaten the viability of this species, especially where cheetahs are pushed to the edge of suitable habitat and prey on domestic animals such as cattle and sheep.

At the turn of the century, an estimated 100,000 cheetahs lived in 44 countries throughout Africa and Asia. Today there are fewer than 12,000 cheetahs worldwide, the majority in a handful of countries in Central and Southern Africa.

The fastest mammal on earth, the cheetah can reach speeds of up to 70 miles per hour. Unfortunately, it has not been able to outrun man.

The encroachment on the cheetah's range as a result of increased numbers of farms and ranches, has dramatically reduced their habitat. Continuing conflict arises as cheetahs find domesticated animals easier prey than a wild duiker or springbok. This has led to indiscriminate killing of cheetahs by ranchers protecting their livestock, which has further depleted wild cheetah populations.

(OPPOSITE) A few minutes after sunrise, a cheetah recovers from a missed attempt at an impala kill. The steam from its body is evidence of the extreme amount of heat generated during a short burst of speed.

Baboons (ABOVE) *live in highly structured units called* **troops.** *As is the case with many monkeys, these primates are experiencing conflict as agricultural growth continues to destroy their natural habitat. Baboons are exterminated when they start raiding croplands in search of food. Although all species of baboons are designated as near threatened by the IUCN, they continue to be hunted for food and sport.* (OPPOSITE) *Chacma baboon.*

(OPPOSITE, BOTTOM) All species of colobus monkey are listed as threatened. The decline of this species was caused initially by the international fur trade in the nineteenth century and later by rapid human population growth and destruction of the monkeys' habitat. The black and white colobus is among the most threatened primate species in Africa. (ABOVE AND OPPOSITE, TOP) Contrary to the colobus, the vervet, or green monkey seems to be adaptable to the presence of human activity. Populations in Africa have remained somewhat stable in spite of continued human development.

(ABOVE AND OPPOSITE) Chimpanzee. Loss of habitat due to agricultural development and logging, hunting by people for food and protection of crops, and commercial exploitation for animal trade, have all significantly reduced numbers of chimpanzees in the wild, and left remaining populations fragmented.

The mountain gorilla (PAGES 332–338) is the world's largest living primate and is one of the most endangered. Although protected within three national parks, they remain entirely surrounded by dense human and agricultural developments. The increase in human demand for natural resources conflicts with preservation efforts and continues to place pressure on remaining gorilla populations.

The most endangered of the three gorilla subspecies in Africa is the mountain gorilla. Scientists estimate that only about 600 of these animals survive in the forests of Rwanda, Uganda and the New Democratic Congo.

The International Gorilla Conservation Programme was established to provide critical protection for gorillas. Part of the protection effort includes the creation of a viable economy for the local inhabitants, to prevent further degradation of the surrounding gorilla habitat. Through a combination of international efforts, programs are currently in place, allowing local communities to share in the benefits of gorilla-based tourism. A system of this type has also provided operating revenue for the Uganda Wildlife Authority.

The International Gorilla Conservation Programme is also involved with implementing training programs for dealing with gorillas raiding croplands bordering the park. These human-gorilla (HUGO) conflict/response teams are trained to "herd" the gorillas back into the forest before conflicts create serious problems. Community-park teams like these allow for joint problem-solving efforts between the communities and the park, strengthening the relationship between the two groups.

Atrocities perpetrated against the mountain gorilla have been severe. In the 1970's, these primates were massacred exclusively for their heads. In 1984, civil war continued to reduce the remaining populations. Although use in traditional remedies is not as prevalent as with other animals, gorilla bones are sometimes used for medicinal purposes, thus further contributing to the demise of the species.

Man is one of over 4,000 species of mammals in existence today. Humanity's superiority over other mammals is a result of our intelligence and ability to demonstrate a moral conscience. Yet, we are the only mammal on earth that has developed the technology and possesses the power to destroy all forms of life on our planet. We must find a way to use our unique abilities for the benefit — not detriment — of the preservation of our natural resources. In our lifetime, we hold an obligation greater than our forefathers and no less than the generation which will follow. Our current actions may well set us on an irreversible course of destruction if we do not value our human and ecological resources differently than in the past. The success of this century will be measured by our priorities and actions. We cannot afford to fail.

—Howard G. Buffett